clock
reloj

rocket
cohete

ENGLISH
—and—
SPANISH
My First 1000 Words

Illustrated by Judy Hensman

butterfly
mariposa

tractor
tractor

parrot
loro

flower
flor

father
padre

mother
madre

brother
hermano

sister
hermana

Brown Watson
ENGLAND

contents: índice

ISBN 0-7097-1191-3
First published 1997 by Brown Watson
The Old Mill, 76 Fleckney Road
Kibworth Beauchamp, Leicestershire, England
© 1997 Brown Watson
Printed in the E.C.

father, husband
padre, marido

grandfather
abuelo

mother, wife
madre, esposa

grandmother
abuela

son, brother
hijo, hermano

daughter, sister
hija, hermana

cousin
prima

cousin
primo

aunt
tía

uncle
tío

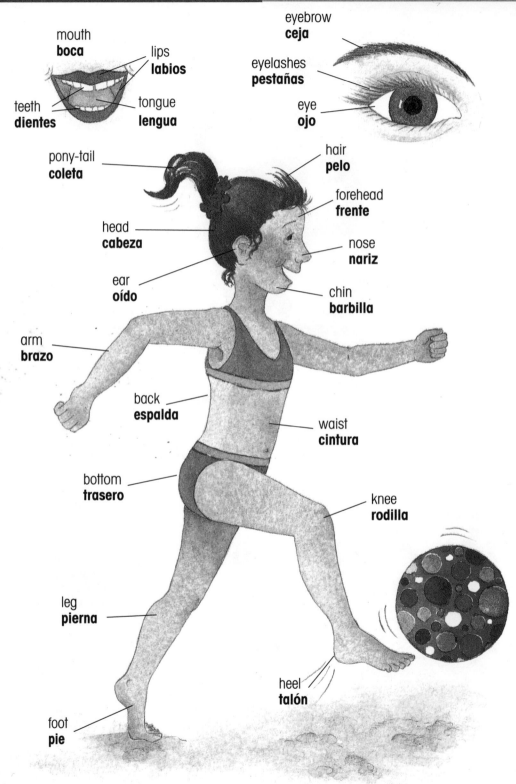

eyebrow
ceja

mouth
boca

lips
labios

eyelashes
pestañas

teeth
dientes

tongue
lengua

eye
ojo

pony-tail
coleta

hair
pelo

forehead
frente

head
cabeza

nose
nariz

ear
oído

chin
barbilla

arm
brazo

back
espalda

waist
cintura

bottom
trasero

knee
rodilla

leg
pierna

heel
talón

foot
pie

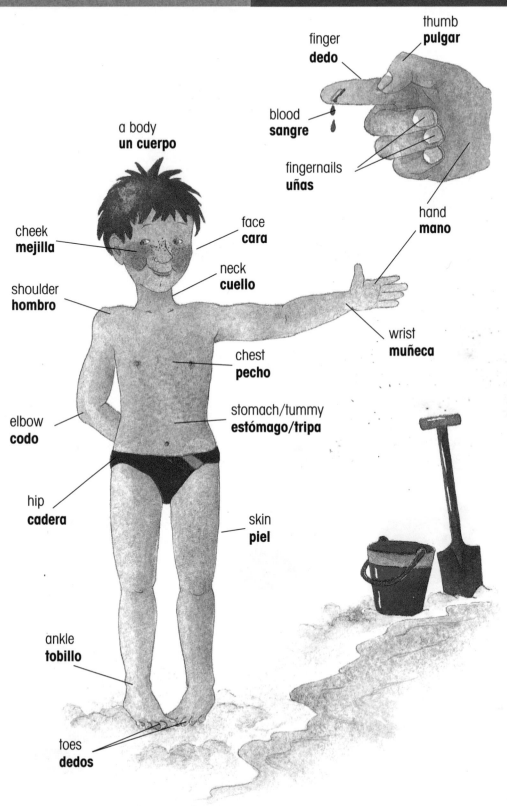

thumb
pulgar

finger
dedo

blood
sangre

fingernails
uñas

a body
un cuerpo

hand
mano

cheek
mejilla

face
cara

neck
cuello

shoulder
hombro

wrist
muñeca

chest
pecho

stomach/tummy
estómago/tripa

elbow
codo

hip
cadera

skin
piel

ankle
tobillo

toes
dedos

5

more words

bald
calva

people
personas

parents
padres

moustache
bigote

beard
barba

man
hombre

boy
niño

bride
novia

hear
oír

taste
saborear

twins
gemelas

bridegroom
novio

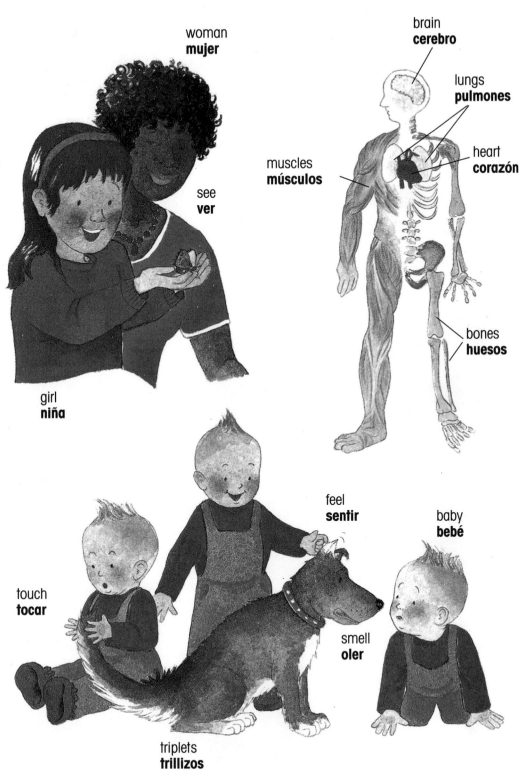

woman
mujer

brain
cerebro

lungs
pulmones

muscles
músculos

see
ver

heart
corazón

bones
huesos

girl
niña

feel
sentir

baby
bebé

touch
tocar

smell
oler

triplets
trillizos

7

clothes

sweater
jersey

hat
sombrero

knickers
braguitas

dressing gown
bata

trousers
pantalón

dress
vestido

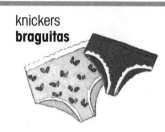

anorak
anorak

socks
calcetines

blouse
blusa

skirt
falda

pyjamas
pijama

petticoat
combinación

leggings
leotardos

coat
abrigo

cap
gorra

8

ropa

shorts
bermudas

raincoat
impermeable

T-shirt
polo

tights
medias

vest
camiseta

jacket
chaqueta

nightdress
camisón

jeans
vaqueros

scarf
bufanda

underpants
calzoncillos

cardigan
chaqueta de punto

rainhat
gorro de lluvia

pullover
suéter

shirt
camisa

track suit
chándal

9

laces
cordones

slippers
zapatillas

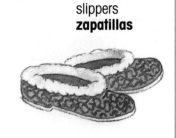

earrings
pendientes

tie
corbata

buttonhole
ojal

handkerchief
pañuelo

braces
tirantes

button
botón

suit
traje

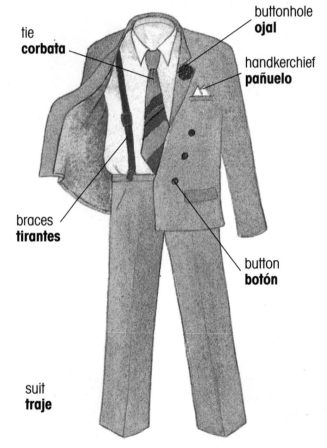

necklace
collar

rubber boots
botas de agua

glasses
gafas

shoes
zapatos

mittens
manoplas

apron
delantal

overalls
mono

gloves
guantes

ring
anillo

athletic shoes
deportivas

belt
cinturón

boots
botas

buckle
hebilla

tiara
diadema

swimsuit
traje de baño

ribbon
lazo

hairband
cinta

sandals
sandalias

bracelet
pulsera

brooch
broche

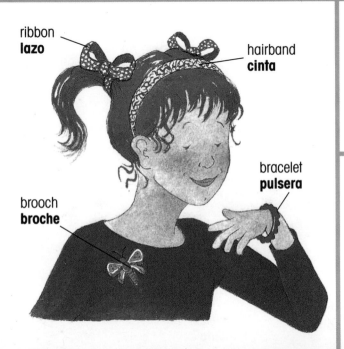

swimtrunks
bañador

bedside table
mesilla

lamp
lámpara

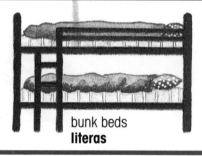

bunk beds
literas

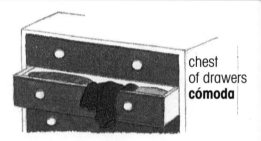

chest
of drawers
cómoda

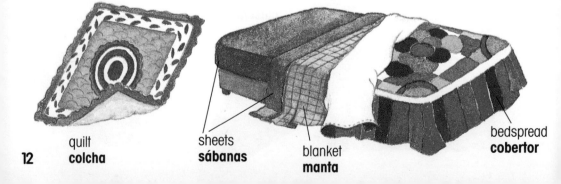

quilt
colcha

sheets
sábanas

blanket
manta

bedspread
cobertor

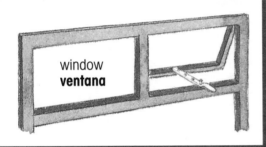
window
ventana

curtains
cortinas

alarm clock
despertador

wardrobe
ropero

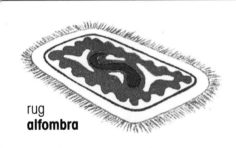
rug
alfombra

bed
cama

cot
cuna

pillow
almohada

duvet
edredón

cradle
cuna-mecedora

the bathroom

plug-hole
desagüe

plug
tapón

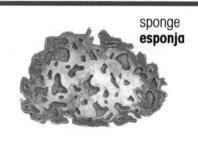

sponge
esponja

bath
bañera

bubbles
burbujas

toilet
retrete

toilet paper
papel higiénico

wash-basin
lavabo

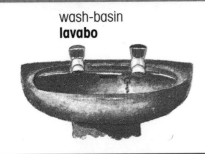

towel
toalla

shower-curtain
cortina de ducha

bidet
bidé

towel-rail
toallero

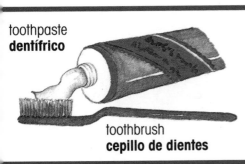

soap
jabón

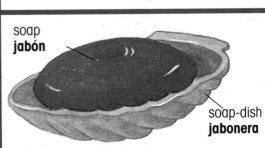

soap-dish
jabonera

toothpaste
dentífrico

toothbrush
cepillo de dientes

shower
ducha

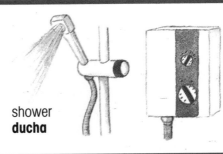

tap
grifo

potty
orinal

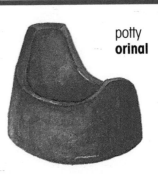

15

food-mixer
batidora

kettle
hervidor

coffee pot
cafetera

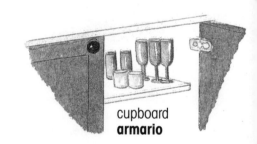

cupboard
armario

stove
cocina

oven
horno

draining board
escurridor

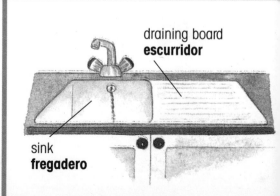

sink
fregadero

teapot
tetera

vacuum cleaner
aspiradora

iron
plancha

ironing board
planchero

washing machine

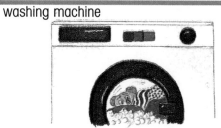

lavadora

dish-washer
lavaplatos

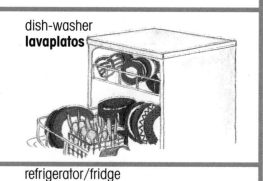

switch
interruptor

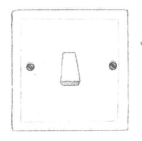

refrigerator/fridge
nevera

socket
enchufe

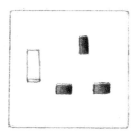

electric plug
clavija

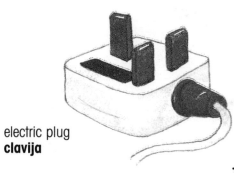

freezer
congelador

books
libros

book-ends
sujeta libros

remote control
mando a distancia

hi-fi system
cadena de música

vase of flowers

florero

door-handle
picaporte

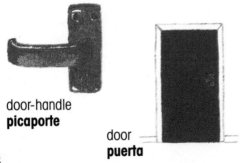

door
puerta

gas fire
estufa

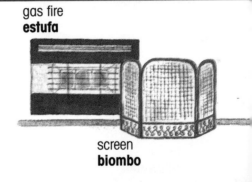

screen
biombo

painting
cuadro

magazine rack
revistero

newspapers
periódicos

comics
tebeos

telephone/phone
teléfono

magazines
revistas

video recorder
reproductor de vídeo

television
set/TV
televisión

video cassette
videocasete

cushions
cojines

photographs
fotografías

mantelpiece
repisa

fireplace
chimenea

radio
radio

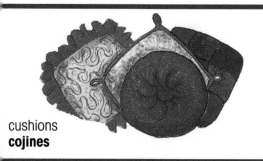

the dining-room

table-cloth

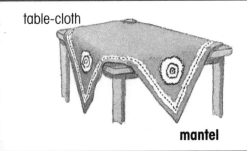

mantel

plates

platos

cup
taza

saucer
platillo

teaspoon
cucharilla

oil
aceitera

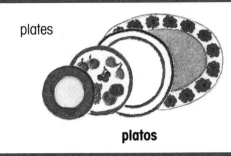

vinegar
vinajera

mirror
espejo

fork
tenedor

spoon
cuchara

place-mat
salvamanteles

napkins
servilletas

napkin ring
servilletero

knife
cuchillo

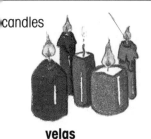

candles

candlestick
candelabro

velas

pepper
pimienta

salt
sal

dining-table
mesa de comedor

chairs
sillas

eggcups
hueveras

jug
jarra

tumbler
vaso

fruit bowl

frutero

wine-glasses

copas de vino

bottle
botella

21

the playroom

toys
JUGUETES

rocking horse
balancín

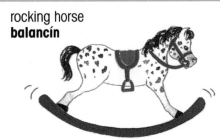

soft toys
peluches

playpen

corral

train set
tren de juguete

building blocks
construcciones

toy soldiers
soldaditos

fort
fuerte

toy duck
pato de juguete

toy boats
barcos de juguete

spinning top
peonza

teddy bear
osito de peluche

toy cars
coches de juguete

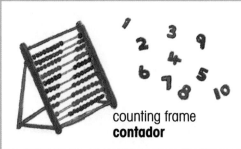

counting frame
contador

skittles
bolos

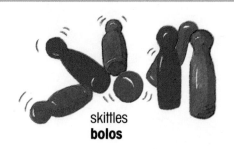

doll's house
casa de muñecas

doll's pram
coche de muñecas

playhouse
cabaña

hatstand
perchero

settee/sofa
sofá

bench
banco

armchair
butaca

footstool
escabel

rug
alfombra

stool
taburete

rocking-chair
mecedora

high-chair
trona

24

cosas de la casa

bookcase
librería

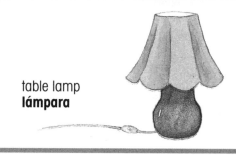

table lamp
lámpara

cupboard
aparador

grandfather clock
reloj de pared

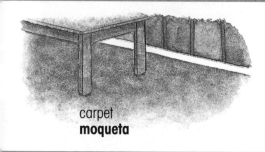

carpet
moqueta

coffee table
mesa auxiliar

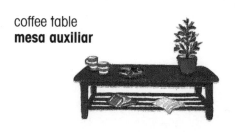

candelabra
candelabro

dressing-table
coqueta

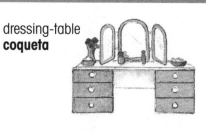

breakfast
desayuno

the garden

greenhouse
invernadero

shed **cobertizo**

hedge
seto

watering-can
regadera

compost
abono

dustbin
cubo

vegetable plot
huerto

rake
rastrillo

garden fork
horca

spade
pala

wheelbarrow
carretilla

sprinkler
aspersor

hoe
azadón

flowers
flores

chimney
chimenea

TV aerial
antena de TV

bonfire
hoguera

roof
tejado

drain-pipe
canalón

porch
entrada

ladder
escalera

front
door
**puerta
principal**

window box
jardinera

barrel
bidón

roof tiles
tejas

grass lawn
césped

path
sendero

lawnmower
segadora

garden hose
manguera

27

in the workshop

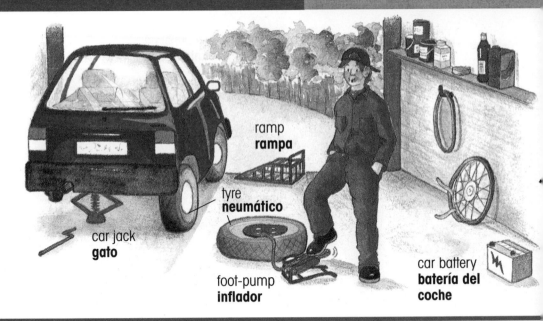

ramp
rampa

tyre
neumático

car jack
gato

foot-pump
inflador

car battery
batería del coche

paint-brushes
pinceles

saw
sierra

sandpaper
papel de lija

paint tins
botes de pintura

nuts and bolts

tornillos/tuercas

file
lima

tools
llaves inglesas

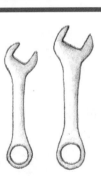

pickaxe
pico

oilcan
aceitera

clamp
torno

axe
hacha

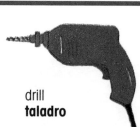
drill
taladro

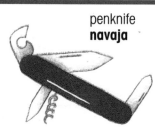
penknife
navaja

wooden plank
tabla de madera

screwdriver
destornillador

screws
tornillos

bucket
cubo

toolbox
caja de herramientas

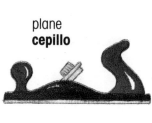
plane
cepillo

hammer
martillo

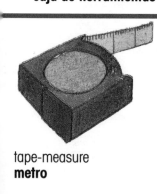
tape-measure
metro

pliers
alicate

nails
clavos

29

mouse
ratón

toad
sapo

hamster
hámster

rat
rata

frog
rana

guinea-pig
conejo de Indias

gerbil
ratón de campo

rabbit
conejo

basket
cesto

cat
gato

tortoise
tortuga

kitten
gatito

fishbowl
pecera

kennel
perrera

newt
tritón

goldfish
pez de colores

terrapin
galápago

puppy
cachorro

hedgehog
puerco espín

dog
perro

silkworm
gusano de seda

stick-insect
insecto

budgie
cotorra

canary
canario

lizard
lagartija

pigeon
paloma

lovebirds
periquito

mynah bird
mirlo

horse
caballo

birdcage
jaula

parrot
loro

foal
potro

Shetland pony
póney

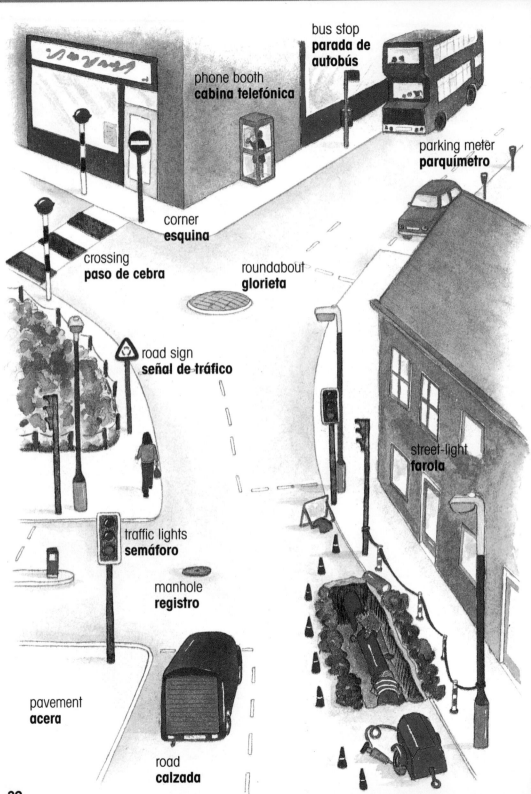

bus stop
parada de autobús

phone booth
cabina telefónica

parking meter
parquímetro

corner
esquina

crossing
paso de cebra

roundabout
glorieta

road sign
señal de tráfico

street-light
farola

traffic lights
semáforo

manhole
registro

pavement
acera

road
calzada

bicycle
bicicleta

bus
autobús

fire-engine
coche de bomberos

taxi
taxi

car
coche

steam-roller
apisonadora

uck
amión

motor-cycle
moto

police car
coche de policía

van **furgoneta**

church
iglesia

restaurant
restaurante

market
mercado

houses
casas

hotel
hotel

skyscraper
rascacielos

post office
correos

shop
tienda

parked cars
aparcamiento

theatre
teatro

34

bank
banco

factory
fábrica

pub
bar

park

parque

school
colegio

supermarket
supermercado

library
biblioteca

cinema
cine

police station
comisaría

office block
oficinas

35

in the supermarket

breakfast cereal
cereales

sausages
salchichas

meat
carne

fruit juice
zumo de fruta

chicken
pollo

eggs
huevos

ham
jamón

jam
mermelada

chocolate bars
chocolate

fish
pescado

turnstile
paso giratorio

cans
latas

36

cheese
queso

butter
mantequilla

milk
leche

credit card
tarjeta de crédito

money
dinero

receipt
cuenta

cash register
caja

check-out desk
mostrador

purse
monedero

shopping bag
bolsa de la compra

handbag
bolso

orange
naranja

grapes
uvas

banana
plátano

cherries
cerezas

lemon
limón

pineapple
piña

apple
manzana

redcurrants
grosellas

plums
ciruelas

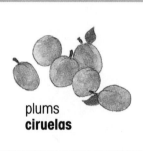

gooseberries
grosellas silvestres

grapefruit
pomelo

pear
pera

melon
melón

strawberries
fresas

blackberries
moras

cabbage
col

tomatoes
tomates

cucumber
pepino

potatoes
patatas

pumpkin
calabaza

peas
guisantes

corn on the cob
mazorca

carrots
zanahorias

onions
cebollas

leeks
puerros

green beans
judías verdes

cauliflower
coliflor

lettuce
lechuga

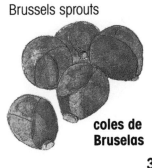

mushrooms
setas

Brussels sprouts

**coles de
Bruselas**

cake
bizcocho

hot dog
perrito caliente

rice
arroz

honey
miel

jelly
gelatina

coconut
coco

toast
tostada

spaghetti
paquete de espaguetis

milk shake
batido

doughnuts
rosquillas

lollipop
polo

sweets
caramelos

fish fingers
barritas de pescado

pancakes
tortitas

soft drink
refresco

más cosas de comer

ice-cream
helado

buns
bollos

sausage roll
empanadilla

nuts
nueces

bag of sugar
paquete de azúcar

chips
patatas fritas

tomato ketchup
salsa de tomate

bar of chocolate
tableta de chocolate

salad
ensalada

apple pie
tarta de manzana

can of soup
bote de sopa

biscuits
galletas

sandwich
emparedado

loaf of bread
pan de molde

pizza
pizza

41

in the park

kite
cometa

railings
verja

picnic
merienda

notice board

bandstand
quiosco de música

scooter
patinete

tablón de anuncios

park keeper
guarda

sand-pit
foso de arena

fountain
fuente

pond
estanque

boats
barcos

swings
columpios

slide
tobogán

see-saw
balancín

roundabout
tiovivo

skipping rope
cuerda

path
camino

drinking fountain
fuente

helmet
casco

roller skates
patines

pads
rodilleras

collar
collar

skateboard
patín

dog muzzle
bozal

43

actor
actor

musician
músico

secretary
secretaria

gardener
jardinero

decorator
pintor

shop-keeper
tendero

astronaut
astronauta

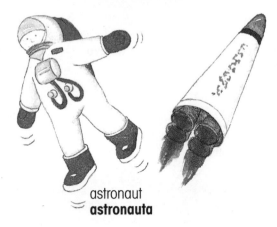

diver
submarinista

cook
cocinero

44

dancer
bailarina

hairdresser
peluquera

singer
cantante

baker
panadero

artist
artista

postman
cartero

farmer
granjero

butcher
carnicero

carpenter
carpintero

45

more people at work

fisherman
pescador

nurse
enfermera

teacher
profesor

miner
minero

waiter
camarero

bricklayer
albañil

plumber
fontanero

explorer
explorador

dentist
dentista

clown
payaso

judge
juez

porter
mozo

TV announcer
locutora

window cleaner
limpiador de cristales

doctor
doctor

fireman
bombero

scientist
científico

electrician
electricista

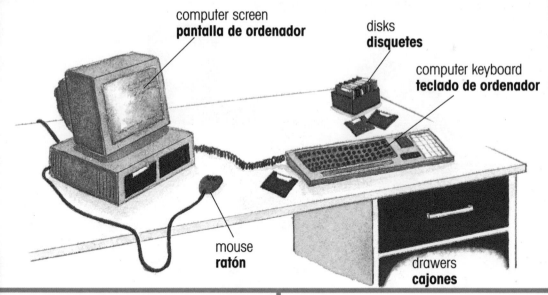

computer screen
pantalla de ordenador

disks **disquetes**

computer keyboard
teclado de ordenador

mouse **ratón**

drawers
cajones

typewriter
**máquina
de escribir**

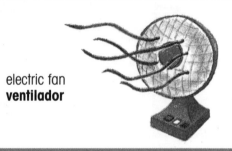

electric fan
ventilador

swivel chair
silla giratoria

fax machine
fax

photocopier
fotocopiadora

writing paper
papel de escribir

envelopes
sobres

calendar
calendario

filing cabinet
archivador

pencil
lápiz

pen
bolígrafo

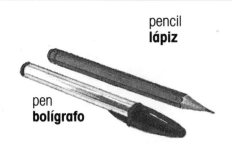

pencil sharpener
sacapuntas

rubber
goma

ruler
regla

stapler
grapadora

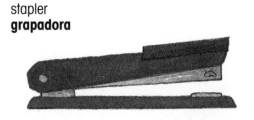

paperweight
pisapapeles

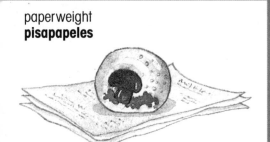

calculator
calculadora

wastepaper bin
papelera

coffee
machine
cafetera

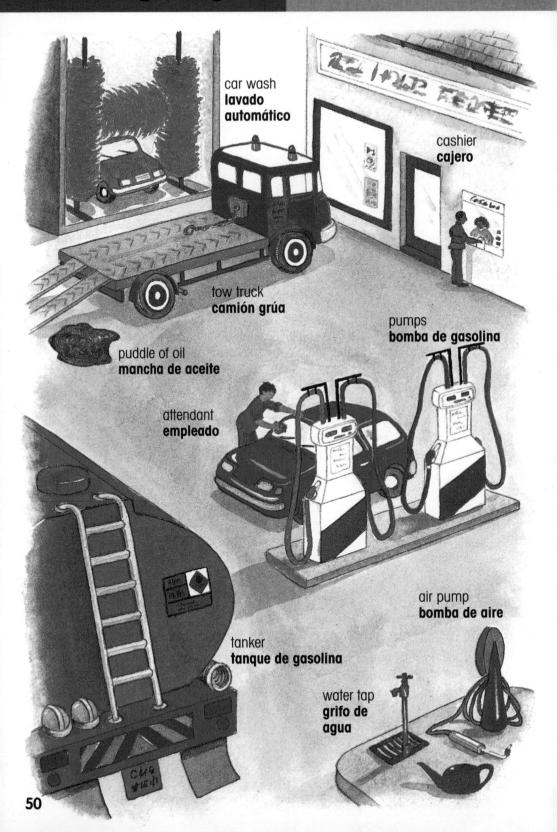

car wash
lavado automático

cashier
cajero

tow truck
camión grúa

pumps
bomba de gasolina

puddle of oil
mancha de aceite

attendant
empleado

air pump
bomba de aire

tanker
tanque de gasolina

water tap
grifo de agua

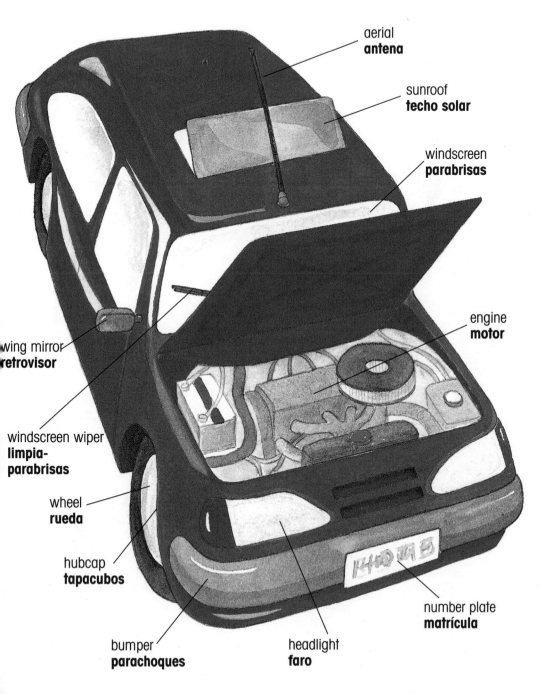

aerial
antena

sunroof
techo solar

windscreen
parabrisas

engine
motor

wing mirror
retrovisor

windscreen wiper
**limpia-
parabrisas**

wheel
rueda

hubcap
tapacubos

number plate
matrícula

bumper
parachoques

headlight
faro

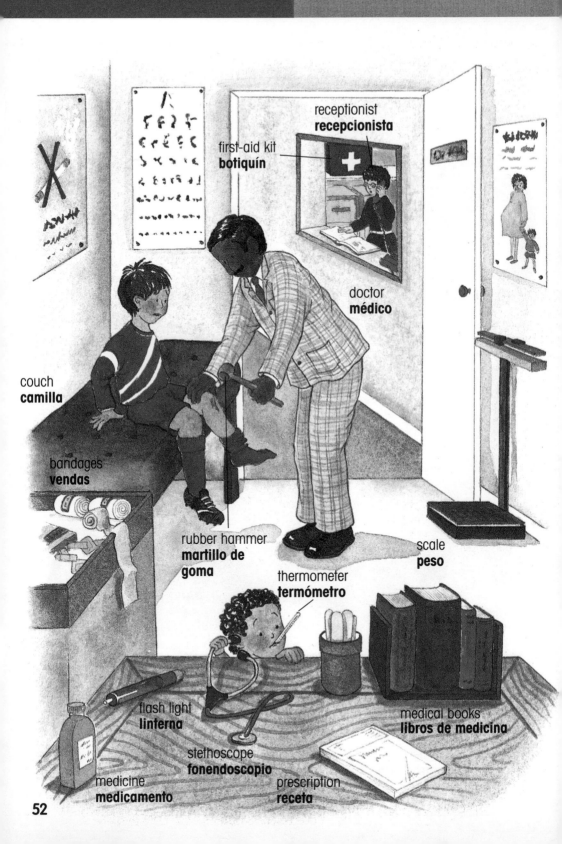

receptionist
recepcionista

first-aid kit
botiquín

doctor
médico

couch
camilla

bandages
vendas

rubber hammer
martillo de goma

thermometer
termómetro

scale
peso

flash light
linterna

medical books
libros de medicina

stethoscope
fonendoscopio

medicine
medicamento

prescription
receta

52

bright light
foco

dentist
dentista

fillings
empastes

dental nurse
enfermera

mask
mascarilla

drill
taladro

glass of mouthwash
vaso de enjuagarse

bib
babero

gown
bata

dentist's mirror
espejos dentales

dentist's chair
silla de dentista

false teeth
dentadura postiza

ambulance
ambulancia

doctor
doctor

vase of flowers
florero

crutches
muletas

glass of orange juice
zumo de naranja

locker
mesilla

cast
escayola

hospital bed
cama de hospital

orderly
camillero

wheelchair
silla de ruedas

bedpan
batea

trolley
carro

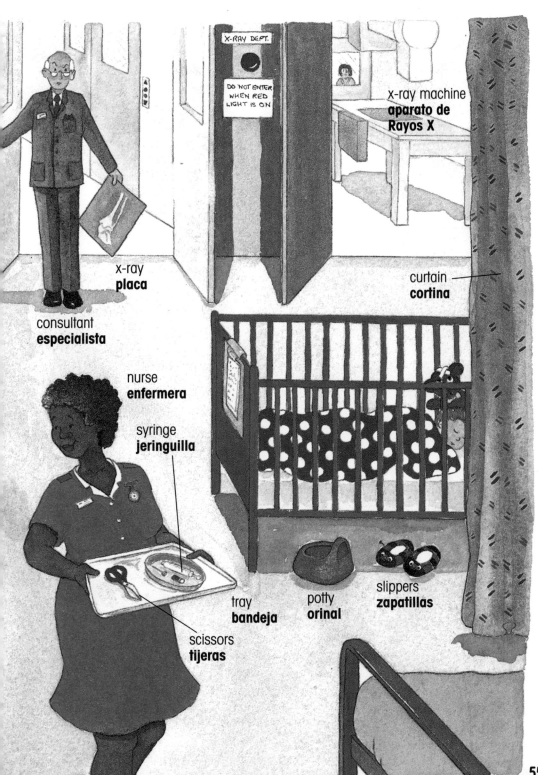

x-ray machine
aparato de Rayos X

x-ray
placa

curtain
cortina

consultant
especialista

nurse
enfermera

syringe
jeringuilla

tray
bandeja

potty
orinal

slippers
zapatillas

scissors
tijeras

X-RAY DEPT.

DO NOT ENTER WHEN RED LIGHT IS ON

55

games and pastimes

reading
leer

writing
escribir

blindman's buff
la gallinita ciega

dressing-up
disfrazarse

sewing
coser

singing
cantar

board game
juegos de mesa

collecting stamps
coleccionar sellos

sleeping
dormir

chess
ajedrez

computer games
juegos de ordenador

walking
pasear

listening to music
escuchar música

dancing
bailar

playing cards
jugar a las cartas

leapfrog
pídola

gardening
cuidar el jardín

making music
tocar música

sports

canoeing
piragüismo

American football
fútbol americano

diving
saltos de trampolín

tennis
tenis

showjumping
saltos de competición

basketball
baloncesto

skating
patinaje

rugby
rugby

cycling
ciclismo

swimming
natación

gymnastics
gimnasia

skiing
esquí

baseball
béisbol

cricket
cricket

table tennis
ping-pong

running
correr

soccer
fútbol

horse-riding
**montar a
caballo**

sheep
oveja

lamb
cordero

calf
ternero

cow
vaca

ducklings.
patitos

duck
pato

milk
containers
lecheras

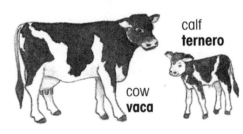

orchard
frutales

cockerel
gallo

haystack
paja

turkey
pavo

goslings
gansitos

goose
ganso

horse
caballo
foal
potro
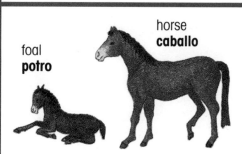

bull
toro

tractor
tractor

goat
cabra
kid
cabrito
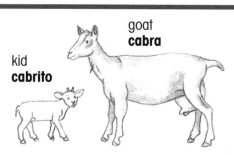

pig
cerdo
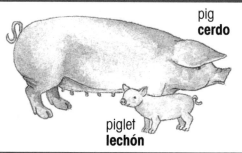
piglet
lechón

hen
gallina
chicks
polluelos

field
campo
fence
cercado
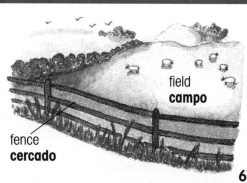

61

lunch-box
merienda

pupils
alumnos

globe
bola del mundo

pot of
paste
**cubo de
engrudo**

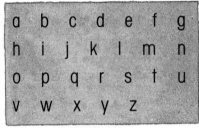

alphabet
abecedario

slide projector
proyector

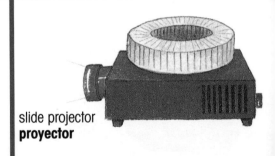

wall chart
póster

teacher
profesora

blackboard
pizarra

easel
caballete

notebook
cuaderno

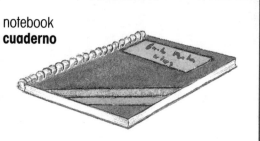

school bag
cartera

duster
borrador

chalks
tizas

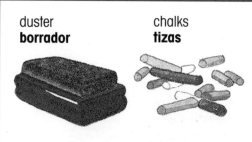

drawing
dibujo

pencil case
plumier

modelling clay
arcilla

writing
redacción

63

going by train

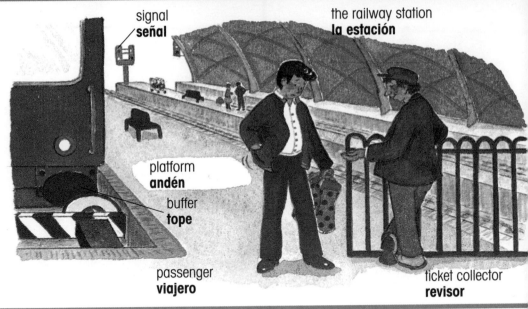

signal
señal

the railway station
la estación

platform
andén

buffer
tope

passenger
viajero

ticket collector
revisor

escalator
escaleras mecánicas

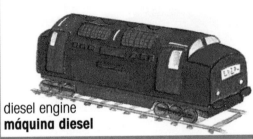

diesel engine
máquina diesel

level crossing
paso a nivel

passenger car

railway line
vía del tren

freight car
vagón de mercancías

vagón de pasajeros

viajando en tren

ticket office
venta de billetes

dining car
coche restaurante

Dining Car / coche restaurante

porter
maletero

luggage
equipaje

tunnel
túnel

underground railway   **metro**

monorail

monorraíl

signal box
cuadro de mandos

smoke
humo

steam engine   **máquina de vapor**   65

going by water

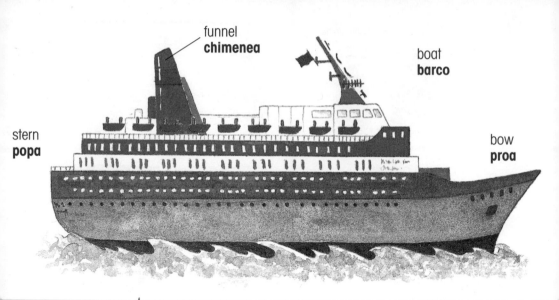

funnel
chimenea

boat
barco

stern
popa

bow
proa

tug-boat
remolcador

mast
mástil

yacht
yate

submarine
submarino

anchor
ancla

buoy
boya

hydrofoil
hidroplano

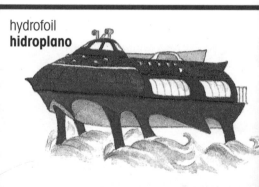

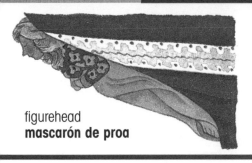

figurehead
mascarón de proa

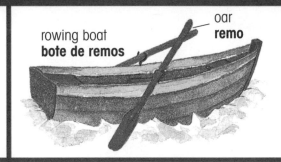

rowing boat
bote de remos

oar
remo

barge
gabarra

hovercraft **aerodeslizador**

paddle-
steamer
barco de vapor

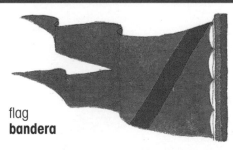

flag
bandera

speedboat
lancha rápida

ferry-boat
transbordador

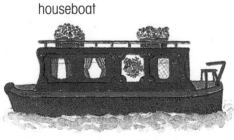

houseboat

casa flotante

sails
velas

67

going by plane

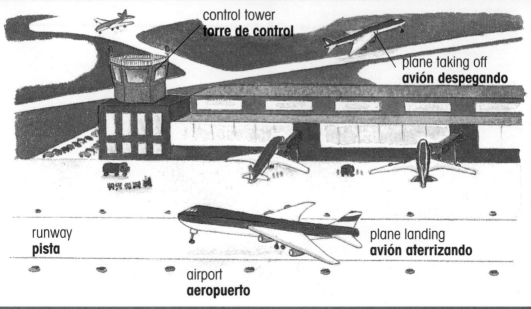

control tower
torre de control

plane taking off
avión despegando

runway
pista

plane landing
avión aterrizando

airport
aeropuerto

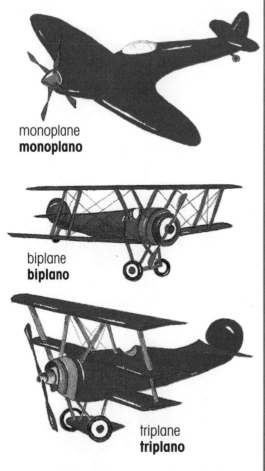

monoplane
monoplano

biplane
biplano

triplane
triplano

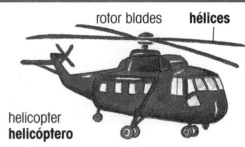

rotor blades **hélices**

helicopter
helicóptero

fuel tanker
tanque de gasóleo

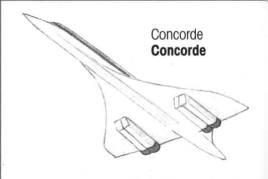

Concorde
Concorde

air hostess
azafata

seaplane
hidroavión

passenger jet
avión de reacción

light aircraft
avioneta

glider
planeador

jumbo jet
avión de pasajeros

tail
cola

cockpit
cabina

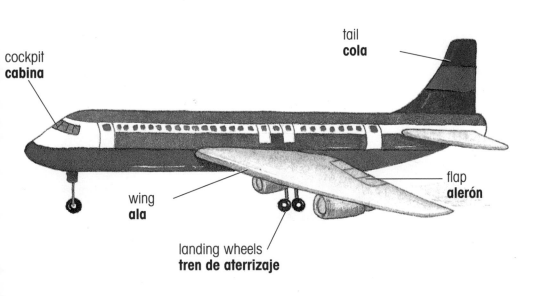

flap
alerón

wing
ala

landing wheels
tren de aterrizaje

69

in the country

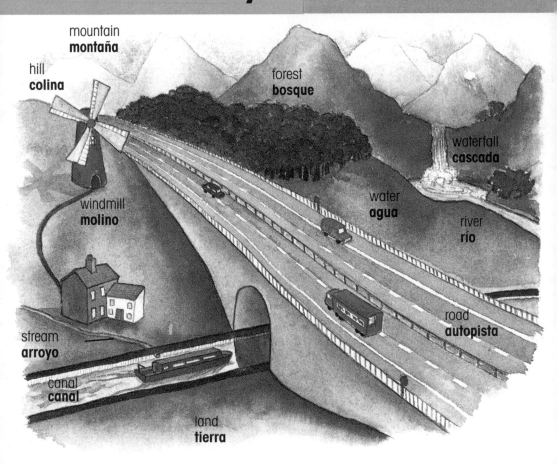

mountain
montaña

hill
colina

forest
bosque

waterfall
cascada

windmill
molino

water
agua

river
río

stream
arroyo

road
autopista

canal
canal

land
tierra

rocks
rocas

hiker
excursionista

map
mapa

caravan
caravana

tent
tienda de campaña

camper
campista

campfire
fogata

sleeping bag
saco de dormir

fishing rod
caña

fishing net
red de pescar

fisherman
pescador

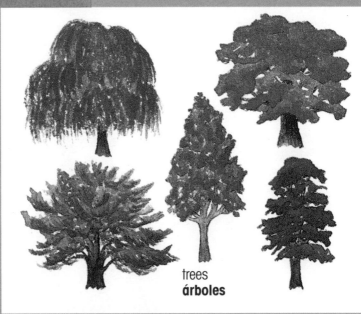

trees
árboles

scarecrow

espantapájaros

wild flowers
flores silvestres

stream

arroyo

village
aldea

town
ciudad

city
ciudad

builders and buildings

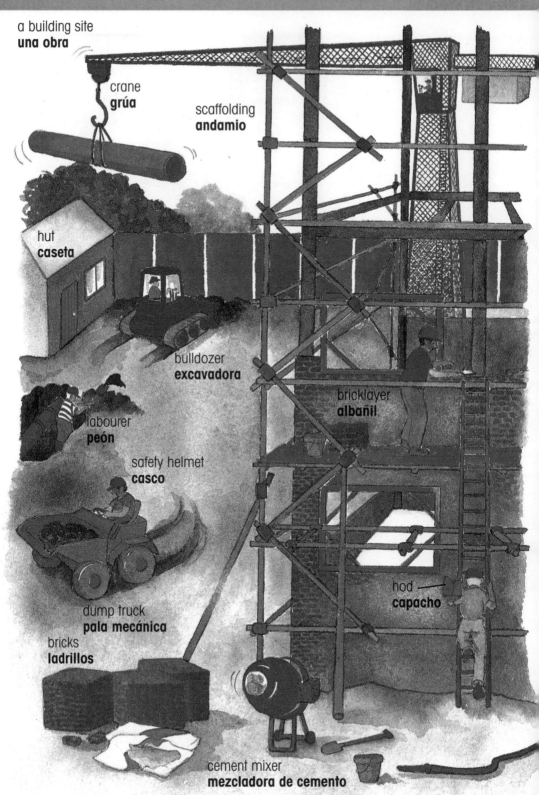

a building site
una obra

crane
grúa

scaffolding
andamio

hut
caseta

bulldozer
excavadora

labourer
peón

bricklayer
albañil

safety helmet
casco

hod
capacho

dump truck
pala mecánica

bricks
ladrillos

cement mixer
mezcladora de cemento

fire station
estación de bomberos

houses
manzana de casas

cottage
chalet

mosque

mezquita

car park
aparcamiento

hospital
hospital

art gallery
galería de arte

hangar
hangar

castle   **castillo**

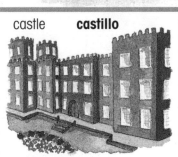

boathouse   **cobertizo para barcas**

museum
museo

tower
torre

winter
invierno

spring
primavera

lightning
relámpago

sunshine
sol

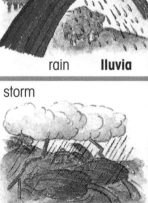

autumn
otoño

rainbow
arco iris

rain **lluvia**

storm

tormenta

summer **verano**

hail
granizo

ice
hielo

snow
nieve

animalitos pequeños

cobweb
telaraña

ladybird
mariquita

spider
araña

beetle
escarabajo

snail
caracol

centipede
ciempiés

praying mantis
mantis religiosa

earwig
tijereta

wasp
avispa

scorpion
escorpión

caterpillar
oruga

bee
abeja

beehive
colmena

chrysalis
crisálida

butterfly
mariposa

slug
babosa

75

peacock
pavo real

owl
búho

monkey
mono

ostrich
avestruz

tiger
tigre

giraffe
jirafa

lion
león

elephant
elefante

gorilla
gorila

penguin
pingüino

woodpecker
pájaro carpintero

stork
cigüeña

swan
cisne

porcupine
puerco espín

panda
oso panda

crocodile
cocodrilo

zebra
cebra

rhinoceros/rhino
rinoceronte

hippopotamus/hippo
hipopótamo

whale
ballena

octopus
pulpo

dolphin
delfín

lobster
langosta

swordfish
pez espada

manta ray
manta raya

moose
alce

shark
tiburón

camel
camello

polar bear
oso polar

platypus
ornitorrinco

armadillo
armadillo

kangaroo
canguro

seahorse
**caballito
de mar**

leopard
leopardo

koala
koala

sloth
perezoso

cobra
cobra

boa constrictor
boa constrictor

seal
foca

walrus
morsa

wing
ala

feather
pluma

antlers
cornamenta

beak
pico

tail
cola

whiskers
bigotes

paw
zarpa

fin
aleta dorsal

hoof
pezuña

flipper
aleta

shell
concha

pouch
bolsa marsupial

hump
joroba

tusk
colmillo

trunk
trompa

plantas

plants

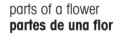

parts of a flower
partes de una flor

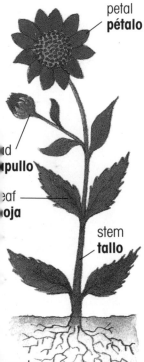

petal **pétalo**

d
pullo

eaf
oja

stem **tallo**

roots
raíces

holly
acebo

cactus
cactus

seeds

semillas

shoots
retoños

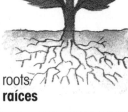

rushes
juncos

bush
arbusto

creeper
enredadera

bulb
bulbo

wheat
trigal

indoor plant
planta de interior

bramble
zarza

twig **brote**

branch
rama

trunk
tronco

81

seagulls **gaviotas**

water-skiing **esquí acuático**

donkey **burro**

windsurfer **winsurfista**

crab **cangrejo**

mussels **mejillones**

shellfish **conchas**

jellyfish **medusa**

seaweed **algas**

pool **poza**

starfish **estrella de mar**

sandcastle **castillo de arena**

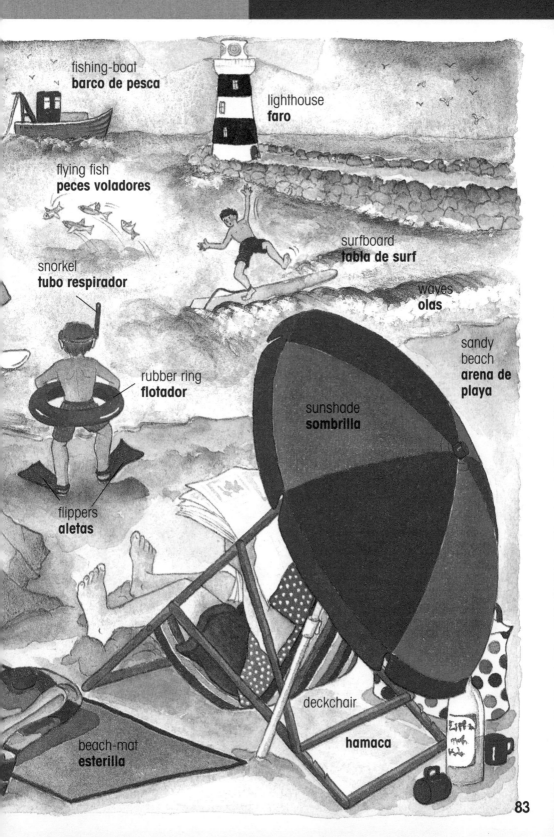

fishing-boat
barco de pesca

lighthouse
faro

flying fish
peces voladores

surfboard
tabla de surf

snorkel
tubo respirador

waves
olas

sandy
beach
**arena de
playa**

rubber ring
flotador

sunshade
sombrilla

flippers
aletas

deckchair

beach-mat
esterilla

hamaca

paper chain
guirnalda

birthday cards
felicitaciones

balloons
globos

cloak
capa

candles
velas

paper hat
gorro de papel

cake
tarta

sweets
caramelos

biscuits
galletas

sandwiches
sándwiches

crackers
petardos

fizzy drinks
bebidas

chocolates
bombones

straws
pajas

crumbs
migas

84

sparklers
bengalas

magician
mago

party invitation
invitación

Please come to my fancy dress party

hostess
anfitriona

guest
invitado

presents
regalos

ribbon
lazo

fancy dress costumes
disfraces

85

opposites

over
sobre

in
dentro

out
fuera

under
debajo

up
arriba

down
abajo

happy
feliz

sad
triste

high
alto

wet
mojado

dry
seco

low
bajo

fast
rápido

thin
delgado

fat
gordo

slow
lento

big
grande

above
encima

small
pequeño

below
debajo

in front
delante

behind
detrás

palabras de cuentos storybook words

ghost
fantasma

witch
bruja

pirate
pirata

dwarf
enano

fairy
hada

dragon
dragón

giant
gigante

wizard
hechicero

mermaid
sirena

dinosaur
dinosaurio

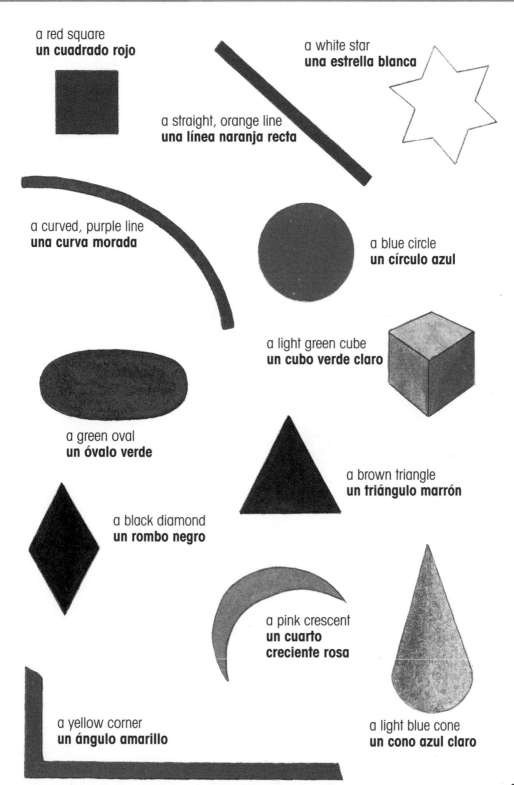

a red square
un cuadrado rojo

a white star
una estrella blanca

a straight, orange line
una línea naranja recta

a curved, purple line
una curva morada

a blue circle
un círculo azul

a light green cube
un cubo verde claro

a green oval
un óvalo verde

a brown triangle
un triángulo marrón

a black diamond
un rombo negro

a pink crescent
**un cuarto
creciente rosa**

a yellow corner
un ángulo amarillo

a light blue cone
un cono azul claro

89

1 one girl
una niña

2 two boys
dos niños

3 three ponies
tres potros

4 four cows
cuatro vacas

5 five puppies
cinco cachorros

6 six kittens
seis gatos

7 seven lambs
siete ovejas

8 eight pigs
ocho cerdos

9 nine ducks
nueve patos

10 ten mice
diez ratones

English words in this book/palabras inglesas de este libro